HOME FIRES

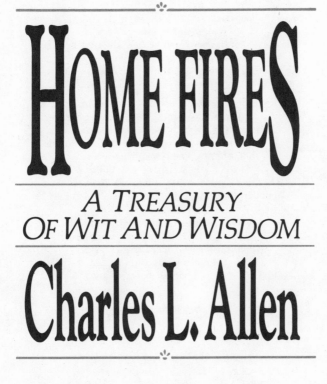

HOME FIRES

A TREASURY OF WIT AND WISDOM

Charles L. Allen

WORD BOOKS
PUBLISHER
WACO, TEXAS

A DIVISION OF
WORD, INCORPORATED

HOME FIRES: A TREASURY OF WIT AND WISDOM

Unless otherwise noted, Scripture quotations are from
The King James Version of the Bible. Other Scripture
quotations are from the following sources:
The New Testament in Modern English by J. B. Phillips,
published by The Macmillan Company,
© 1958, 1960, 1972 by J. B. Phillips.
The New American Standard Bible, © The Lockman
Foundation 1960, 1962, 1963, 1968, 1971, 1972, 1973,
1975, 1977.
A New Translation of the Bible by James Moffatt.
Copyright © 1954 by James Moffatt.
Published by Harper & Row Publishers
and Hodder and Stoughton, Ltd.
Further acknowledgments appear on pp. 126–127.

Library of Congress Cataloging in Publication Data:

Home fires.

1. Homiletical illustrations.   I. Allen, Charles
Livingstone, 1913–   .
BV4225.2.H65   1987   242   87-14662
ISBN 0-8499-0610-5

Printed in the United States of America

7 8 9 8 FG 9 8 7 6 5 4 3 2 1

CONTENTS

❧

I

~

Homes are the building blocks of civilization.

ARNOLD J. TOYNBEE

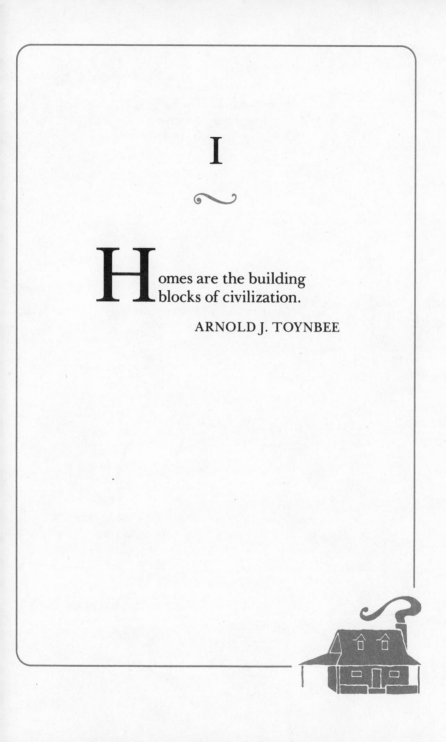

The family, as far as I'm concerned, is the whole bag. I've never lost my own sense of family. It's all I've ever really cared about.

HOWARD COSELL

~

A house is built of logs and stone,
Of tiles and posts and piers;
A home is built of loving deeds
That stand a thousand years.

VICTOR HUGO

~

What is wealth? Money—or what's worth money? Would you take a million dollars for your health, or your eyesight, or your wife and children? Certainly not! Well, then, what do you mean by complaining of having too little? Good heavens, man, you're a millionaire!

CHANNING POLLOCK

The ultimate economic and spiritual unit of any civilization is still the family.

CLARE BOOTH LUCE

∽

When my son Danny was a four-year-old, we lived in a trailer. One day someone asked him, "Don't you wish you had a real home?"

I was really proud when I heard him reply, "We have a real home; we just don't have a house to put it in."

MRS. E. MILLER
Guideposts

∽

Six things are requisite to create a "happy home":
Integrity must be the architect—
Tidiness the upholsterer—
It must be warmed by affection—
Lighted up with cheerfulness—
Industry must be the ventilation—
Over all, as a protecting canopy and glory, nothing will suffice except the blessing of God.

HAMILTON

HOME

"What makes a home?"
I asked my little boy.
And this is what he said,
"You, Mother,
And when Father comes,
Our table set all shiny,
And my bed,
And, Mother, I think it's home,
Because we love each other."
You who are old and wise,
What would you say
If you were asked the question?
Tell me, pray.
Thus, simply as a little child, we learn
A home is made from love.
Warm as the golden hearthfire on the floor,
A table and a lamp for light,
And smooth white beds at night—
Only the old sweet fundamental things.
And long ago I learned—
Home may be near, home may be far,
But it is anywhere that love
And a few plain household treasures are.

AUTHOR UNKNOWN

He is happiest, be he king or peasant, who finds peace in his home.

JOHANN WOLFGANG VON GOETHE

The walls of a house are not built of wood, brick or stone, but of truth and loyalty.

Unpleasant sounds, the friction of living, the clash of personalities, are not deadened by Persian rugs or polished floors, but by conciliation, concession and self-control. . . .

The house is not a structure where bodies meet, but a hearthstone upon which flames mingle, separate flames of souls, which, the more perfectly they unite, the more clearly they shine and the straighter they rise toward heaven.

The beauty of a house is harmony.

The security of a house is loyalty.

The joy of a house is love.

The plenty of a house is in children.

The rule of a house is service.

The comfort of a house is in contented spirits.

The maker of a house, of a real human house, is God himself, the same who made the stars and built the world.

DR. FRANK CRANE

11

Every house where love abides
And friendship is a guest,
Is surely home, and home, sweet home
For there the heart can rest.

HENRY VAN DYKE

The family is a school of mutual help. Each member depends on every other. Today the robust father holds the "wee laddie" on his knees, or leads him up the stairway of that schoolroom in which he is to be taught his alphabet. But there is a tomorrow coming by and by when the lisper of the ABC will be the master of a home of his own—with an infirm, gray-haired parent dozing away his sunset years in an armchair. Each helps the other when and where the help is most needed. And every word and deed of unselfish love, comes back in blessings on its author. God puts helpless babes, and infirm parents into our families for this purpose (among others) that the strong may bear the burden of the weak, and in bearing them may grow stronger themselves in Bible graces.

CUYLER

Go home to your family, and tell them what the Lord has done for you, and how he has shown you mercy.

MARK 5:19
R. A. Torrey translation

❧

A family altar would alter a family.

❧

A religious family has been described as one where the father says grace before every meal, and the mother says "Amen" when the football game is over.

❧

Keep far our foes, give peace at home;
Where thou art guide, no ill can come.

1662 ANGLICAN PRAYER BOOK

It is easy to govern a kingdom, but difficult to rule one's family.

~

It's hard to raise a family—especially in the morning.

~

I don't have to look up my family tree, because I know that I'm the sap.

FRED ALLEN

~

A man's home can be his hassle.

DWAIN A. BASS

T he Ten Commandments of human relations are:
(1) Speak to people. There is nothing as nice as a cheerful word of greeting.

(2) Smile at people. It takes 72 muscles to frown, only fourteen to smile.

(3) Call people by name. The sweetest music to anyone's ears is the sound of his or her own name.

(4) Be friendly and helpful.

(5) Be cordial. Speak and act as if everything you do is a genuine pleasure.

(6) Be genuinely interested in people. You can like almost everybody if you try.

(7) Be generous with praise—cautious with criticism.

(8) Be considerate with the feelings of others. There are usually three sides to a controversy;—yours, the other person's, and the right one.

(9) Be alert to give service. What counts most in life is what we do for others.

(10) Add to this a good sense of humor, a big dose of patience and a dash of humility, and you will be rewarded many fold.

ROBERT G. LEE

Are you willing to stoop down and consider the needs and the desires of little children;

To remember the weakness and loneliness of people who are growing old;

To stop asking how much your friends love you, and ask yourself whether you love them enough;

To bear in mind the things that those who live in the same house with you really want, without waiting for them to tell you;

To trim your lamp so that it will give more light and less smoke, and to carry it in front so that your shadow will fall behind you;

To make a grave for your ugly thoughts, and a garden for your kindly feelings, with the gate open?

HENRY VAN DYKE

Go not abroad for happiness. For see
It is a flower that blooms at thy door.
Bring love and justice home, and then no more
Thou'lt wonder in what dwelling joy may be.

MINOT J. SAVAGE

II

〜

Honor women! They
entwine and weave
heavenly roses in our earthly life.

JOHANN SCHILLER

What is better than gold?
       Jasper.
What is better than jasper?
       Wisdom.
What is better than wisdom?
       Women.
And what is better than a good woman?
       Nothing.

GEOFFREY CHAUCER

❧

A good woman is said to resemble a Cremona
violin—age but increases its worth and
sweetens its tone.

O. W. HOLMES

❧

Twas a woman washed Christ's feet with tears
and a woman that anointed his body to the
burial. There were women that wept when he was
going to the cross and women that followed him
from the cross and that stayed by his sepulchre
when he was buried. They were women that were
first with him at his resurrection morn and women
that brought tidings first to his disciples that he was
risen from the dead. Women therefore are highly
favored.

JOHN BUNYAN
Pilgrim's Progress

Tis beauty, that doth oft make women proud;
'tis virtue, that doth make them most
admired; 'tis modesty, that makes them seem divine.

WILLIAM SHAKESPEARE

Beauty, nobility, wealth, eloquence, appear the
most lovely in these persons that seem not to
know they are endowed with them. Courtesy and
modesty do no way lessen these advantages; but as
they add a grace to them, so they drive away envy.

DESIDERIUS ERASMUS

Your beauty should not be dependent on an
elaborate coiffure, or on the wearing of
jewelry or fine clothes, but on the inner
personality—the unfading loveliness of a calm and
gentle spirit, a thing very precious in the eyes
of God.

1 PETER 3:3–5
J. B. Phillips translation

How goodness heightens beauty!

HANNAH MOORE

If either man or woman would realize the full power of personal beauty, it must be by cherishing noble thoughts and hopes and purposes; by having something to do and something to live for that is worthy of humanity.

UPHAM

❧

Women wish to be loved without a why or a wherefore; not because they are pretty, or good, or well-bred, or graceful, or intelligent, but because they are themselves.

HENRI-FREDERIC AMIEL

❧

O woman! in our hours of ease,
  Uncertain, coy, and hard to please,
And variable as the shade,
By the light quivering aspen made;
When pain and anguish wring the brow,
A ministering angel thou.

SIR WALTER SCOTT

A woman has this quality in common with the angels, that those who suffer belong to her.

HONORÉ DE BALZAC

~

I have often had occasion to remark the fortitude with which women sustain the most overwhelming reverses of fortune. Those disasters which break down the spirit of a man and prostrate him in the dust seem to call forth all the energies of the softer sex and give such intrepidity and elevation to their character, that at times it approaches sublimity.

WASHINGTON IRVING

~

Nature has decreed that the male, generally speaking, is larger and more muscular, so in that sense he is physically stronger, but women are better able to tolerate exposure to heat and cold, starvation, and shock. Women are also less susceptible to baldness, color blindness, skin cysts, stomach ulcers and heart attacks. It is a well known fact that women live longer than men.

There is a genetic rationale for these differences, according to some scientists. Females have two X chromosomes in their sex cells. Males have one X chromosome and one Y chromosome. The Y chromosome is considered inferior.

ANN LANDERS

W hatever women do, they must do twice as well as men to be thought half as good. Luckily, this is not difficult.

CHARLOTTE WHITTON

~

M an's sin is that he has not had enough humility; woman's that she has had too much of it. It is as if, by letting women carry the burden of being humble and pious for them, men have got rid of any need to appropriate these virtues for themselves and so have felt free to visit aggression on the world.

SHEILA D. COLLINS

~

C hange and growth are so basic to adult experience that no woman can automatically view herself as "locked into" a single role or career for her entire life. The courage to change is both active and passive; it is the courage to face and accept changes within ourselves and others and the courage to take risks to change the direction of our lives and work.

PATRICIA WARD AND MARTHA STOUT

A reporter once asked Sir Winston Churchill whether he agreed with the prediction that women would rule the world by the year 2000.

Mr. Churchill's reply was, "Yes, they will still be at it."

❧

M an has his will, but woman has her way.

OLIVER WENDELL HOLMES

❧

W omen will be the weaker sex as long as they're strong enough to get away with it.

FRANKLIN JONES

❧

T here is gladness in her gladness when she is glad;
There is sadness in her sadness when she is sad;
But the gladness in her gladness
And the sadness in her sadness
Are nothing to her madness when she is mad.

SOURCE UNKNOWN

I t is not good for man to be alone; I will make a helper to suit him.

GENESIS 2:18
Moffatt

O n the occasion of his retirement from the Riverside Church, Harry Emerson Fosdick said he had been puzzled all his life by the fact that, on the whole, women have not accomplished as much in a public way as has been accomplished by men. Why is this true? Obviously the brains of women are as good and perhaps better than the brains of men. Yet the sober truth is that there have been relatively few women in the list of composers, artists, scientists, and statesmen. "At last," said Dr. Fosdick, "I know the answer. No woman ever had a wife!"

ELTON AND PAULINE TRUEBLOOD

M ost men could say of their wives the words which are inscribed on the stone to Jennie E. Wilson, died 1882, in the College Hill Cemetery, Lebanon, Illinois:

> She was more to me
> Than I expected.

N o man can live piously or die righteously
without a wife.

JEAN PAUL FRIEDRICH RICHTER

~

A smart wife sees through her husband. A good
wife sees him through.

~

A good woman inspires a man,
A brilliant woman interests him,
A beautiful woman fascinates him—
The sympathetic woman gets him.

HELEN ROWLAND

~

A woman gets angry when a man denies his
faults, because she knew them all along. His
lying mocks her affection; it is the deceit that angers
her more than the faults.

FULTON J. SHEEN

Man cannot degrade woman without himself falling into degradation; he cannot elevate her without at the same time elevating himself.

ALEXANDER WALKER

Womanhood is entitled to the best in manhood. Without it she cannot realize the best in herself.

DR. MAX EXNER

A college professor wrote the words, "woman without her man is a savage" on the board, directing the students to punctuate the sentence correctly.

He found that the males looked at it one way and the females another.

The males wrote: "Woman, without her man, is a savage."

The females wrote: "Woman! Without her, man is a savage."

I'm not denying the women are foolish: God made 'em to match the men.

GEORGE ELIOT

~

A difference between the love of a man and the love of a woman is that a man will always give reasons for loving, but a woman gives no reasons for loving. A man will say, "I love you because you are beautiful; I love you because your teeth are pearly; I love you because you make a good shortening bread; I love you because you are sweet."

The woman just says, "I love you."

FULTON J. SHEEN

~

O ne reason why women are forbidden to preach the gospel is that they would persuade without argument and reprove without giving offence.

JOHN NEWTON

Who can find a virtuous woman? for her price is far above rubies. The heart of her husband doth safely trust in her, so that he shall have no need of spoil. She will do him good and not evil all the days of her life. She seeketh wool, and flax, and worketh willingly with her hands. She is like the merchants' ships; she bringeth her food from afar. She riseth also while it is yet night, and giveth meat to her household, and a portion to her maidens. She considereth a field, and buyeth it; with the fruit of her hands she planteth a vineyard. She girdeth her loins with strength, and strengtheneth her arms. She perceiveth that her merchandise is good: her candle goeth not out by night. She layeth her hands to the spindle, and her hands hold the distaff. She stretcheth out her hand to the poor; yea, she reacheth forth her hands to the needy. She is not afraid of the snow for her household: for all her household are clothed with scarlet. She maketh herself coverings of tapestry; her clothing is silk and purple. Her husband is known in the gates, when he sitteth among the elders of the land. She maketh fine linen, and selleth it; and delivereth girdles unto the merchant. Strength and honor are her clothing; and she shall rejoice in time to come. She openeth her mouth with wisdom; and in her tongue is the law of kindness. She looketh well to the ways of her household, and eateth not the bread of idleness. Her children arise up, and call her blessed; her husband also, and he praiseth her. . . . Favor is deceitful, and beauty is vain: but a woman that feareth the Lord, she shall be praised.

PROVERBS 31:10–30

III

I never met a man I didn't like.

WILL ROGERS

Who dares do all that may become a man, and dares no more, he is a man indeed.

WILLIAM SHAKESPEARE

~

One cannot always be a hero, but one can always be a man.

JOHANN WOLFGANG VON GOETHE

~

Watch ye, stand fast in the faith, quit you like men, be strong.

1 CORINTHIANS 16:13

~

The real man is one who always finds excuses for others but never excuses himself.

HENRY WARD BEECHER

His life was gentle, and the elements
So mix'd in him that Nature might stand up
And say to all the world, "This was a man!"

WILLIAM SHAKESPEARE

A man can never be a true gentleman in manner
until he is a true gentleman at heart.

CHARLES DICKENS

The ideal man bears the accidents of life with
dignity and grace, making the best of the
circumstances.

ARISTOTLE

That best portion of a good man's life,
His little, nameless, unremembered acts
Of kindness and of love.

WILLIAM WORDSWORTH

The measure of a man's real character is what he would do if he knew he would never be found out.

THOMAS BABINGTON MACAULEY

~

There is a very simple test by which we can tell good people from bad; if a smile improves a man's face, he is a good man; if a smile disfigures his face, he is a bad man.

WILLIAM LYON PHELPS

~

I hope I shall always possess firmness and virtue enough to maintain what I consider the most enviable of all titles, the character of an honest man.

GEORGE WASHINGTON

~

Make yourself an honest man, and then you may be sure there is one rascal less in the world.

THOMAS CARLYLE

Until a man has found God, he begins at no beginning and works to no end.

H. G. WELLS

The man who humbly bows before God is sure to walk upright before men.

It doesn't take much of a man to be a Christian—it takes all of him.

DAWSON TROTMAN

In Christian manhood there is no conflict between character and service, for service is one of the essentials of character.

ROBERT E. SPEER

Nothing raises a man to such noble peaks nor drops him into such ashpits of absurdity as the act of falling in love.

RIDGELY HUNT

Recipe for a Good Husband: Be careful in your selection. Do not choose too young, and take only such as have been raised in a good, moral atmosphere. Some wives insist on keeping husbands in a pickle while others keep them in hot water. This only makes them sour, hard and sometimes bitter. Even poor varieties may be made sweet, tender and good by garnishing them with patience—well sweetened with smiles and flavored with kisses. We keep them warm with a steady fire of domestic devotion, and serve with three good meals a day. When thus prepared, they will keep for years.

1915 COOKBOOK

One woman to another: "My husband is absolutely no good at fixing anything, so everything in our house works."

When I haven't helped with a single task,
My wife isn't one bit vexed
Until it occurs to me to ask,
"What can I do for you next?"

THOMAS RUSK

Helping his wife wash the dishes, the Rev. John
Byrnell protested, "This isn't a man's job!"
"Oh yes it is," his wife retorted, quoting
2 Kings 21:13, "I will wipe Jerusalem as a man
wipeth a dish, wiping it, and turning it upside down."

I want a man to do odd jobs about the house, run
on errands—one who never answers back and is
always ready to do my bidding," explained a woman
to an applicant for work.

He replied, "You are looking for a husband,
ma'am, not a hired man."

Women's faults are many; men have only two:
Everything they say and everything they do.

AUTHOR UNKNOWN

∽

They say women talk too much. If you have worked in congress you know that the filibuster was invented by men.

CLARE BOOTH LUCE

∽

A man will laugh at a woman putting on makeup, and then take ten minutes trying to make three hairs on top of his head look like six.

∽

He took his defeat like a man; he blamed it on his wife.

I wonder why people say 'amen' and not 'a women'?" Bobby questioned.

His little friend replied, "Because they sing 'hymns' and not 'hers,' silly."

~

M ama," asked the little girl, "if men go to heaven, too, why don't angels have whiskers?"

"Because, dear," her mother answered, "men get to heaven by a very close shave."

GERTRUDE PIERSON

~

W hen we were young, we resolved not to get married until we met the ideal woman. Years later, we met her, but she was looking for the ideal man.

WEST POINT, MISS., *TIMES-LEADER*

What an absurd thing it is to pass over all the valuable parts of a man, and fix our attention on his infirmities.

JOSEPH ADDISON

~

Consider the hammer—
It keeps its head.
It doesn't fly off the handle.
It keeps pounding away.
It finds the point and then drives it home.
It looks at the other side, too, and then often clinches the matter.
It makes mistakes, but when it does it starts over.
It is the only knocker in the world that does any good.
Men can be good hammers.

SOURCE UNKNOWN

~

All men are born equal, but what they are equal to later on is what counts.

Hurrah for the manly man
Who comes with sunlight on his face,
And the strength to do and the will to dare
And the courage to find the place!

The world delights in the manly man,
And the weak and the evil flee
When the manly man goes forth to hold
His own on land or sea!

SOURCE UNKNOWN

If I were going to pick a single personal qualification that has characterized every man I have seen go to the top, it would be that he was, first and last and above everything else, a man.

When things got tough, when the going got rough, he stood up to it. If things went wrong under his direction, he didn't make excuses. He just went on from there.

LOUIS B. LUNDBORG

It is not what he has, or even what he does, which expresses the worth of a man, but what he is.

HENRI-FREDERIC AMIEL

Nothing is impossible to the man who doesn't have to do it himself.

~

A prominent man was being interviewed by a newspaper reporter. The reporter said, "I understand, sir, that you are a self-made man."

The man turned to the reporter and said slowly, "Yes, I guess I am what you would call a self-made man."

Then he added ruefully, "But if I had it to do over again I think I'd call in a little help."

CHARLES B. TEMPLETON

~

The only social security any able man needs is a good place to work, a good place to worship, and a good home to love.

JAMES J. O'REILLY

No man is really old until his mother stops worrying about him.

WILLIAM RYAN

~

The great man is he who does not lose his child's heart.

~

The Four Ages of Man: (1) The calendar age of life, (2) the physical age of life, (3) the emotional age, (4) the philosophical age.

A man's *calendar* age is beyond his power to alter.

A man's *physical* age is often very much what he makes it.

A man's *emotional* age can often be sadly undeveloped.

The wise man is the man who lives in the *philosophical* age in which he is growing all the time.

THE BRITISH WEEKLY

Some men grow; others just swell.

~

Though his beginnings be but poor and low,
Thank God, a man can grow!

FLORENCE EARL COATES

~

There is nothing noble in being superior to
some other man. The true nobility is in being
superior to your previous self.

HINDU PROVERB

~

God judges a man not by the point he has
reached, but by the way he is faring; not
by distance but by direction.

IV

~

One should believe in marriage as in the immortality of the soul.

HONORÉ DE BALZAC

Where does the family start? It starts with a young man falling in love with a girl—no superior alternative has yet been found.

WINSTON CHURCHILL

~

And Jacob served seven years for Rachel; and they seemed unto him but a few days, for the love he had for her.

GENESIS 29:20

~

Being in love is not looking into another's eyes—it's looking in the same direction.

MRS. DALE CARNEGIE

~

He is half the part of a blessed man,
Left to be finished by such as she.
And she a fair divided excellence;
Whose fullness of perfection lies in him.

WILLIAM SHAKESPEARE

The highest happiness on earth is in marriage. Every man who is happily married is a successful man even if he has failed in everything else.

WILLIAM LYON PHELPS

Marriage is an indissoluble contract in which one party obtains from the other party more than either ever may hope to repay.

O. A. BATTISTA

The goal in marriage is not to think alike, but to think together.

ROBERT C. DODDS

A successful marriage requires falling in love many times, always with the same person.

MIGNON McLAUGHLIN

M arriage is the strictest tie of perpetual friendship, and there can be no friendship without confidence, and no confidence without integrity.

SAMUEL JOHNSON

S ome pray to marry the man they love;
My prayer will somewhat vary;
I humbly pray to heaven above
  That I love the man I marry.

ROSE PASTOR STOKES

M arried people will appreciate the story of how Mrs. Albert Einstein replied to someone who asked her if she understood her husband's theory of relativity.

"No," she said, "I do not understand it. But what is more important to me, I understand Dr. Einstein."

ANSWERS

A man told his wife that on a particular Friday he was going into the boss' office to request the raise that he believed he more than deserved. He was quite nervous and upset. When he finally got his courage to go into the boss' office toward the end of the day, the boss agreed that he deserved the raise and gave him even a larger increase in salary than he had anticipated.

When he arrived home, he noticed the dining room table was set with the best dishes. There were candles burning. His wife was preparing a delicious meal. He thought to himself, "Someone has called her from the office to tell her."

He went into the kitchen, told her the good news, they kissed, and then soon sat down at the table for a delicious meal. Beside his plate was a beautifully lettered note which read: "Congratulations, darling! I knew you'd get the raise. These things will tell you how much I love you."

They enjoyed the delicious meal together. When she got up to get the dessert, he noticed a second card fell from her pocket. He bent over, picked it up, and read: "Don't worry about not getting the raise. You deserved it anyway. These things will tell you how much I love you."

JOE A. HARDING

However important sex instruction may be to marriage, there is one thing more important—*character*. Two people unselfish and considerate, tactful and warmhearted, and salted with humor, who are in love, have the most essential of all qualifications for a successful marriage—they have character.

WILLIAM LYON PHELPS

As to personal tastes, which perhaps form the most serious incompatibility between the sexes, *de gustibus non est disputandum.*

Which being interpreted for the benefit of those who have forgotten Latin, means that there can be no disputing about tastes. It is a shrewd married team that can learn what subjects are not safely debatable.

A minor marital thunderstorm to clear the air may serve a purpose. In the wise policy of God man is born to trouble as the sparks fly upward. But be sure the flying sparks do not kindle into flame. For you cannot insure life's biggest things against fire.

Don't broadcast your differences. If there is a misunderstanding keep it a family secret. Not a breath of it even to your dearest friend. That is the surest way to put the case beyond remedy.

GEORGE W. HUMPHREYS

Success in marriage is more than finding the right person; it is a matter of being the right person.

~

The one word above all others that makes marriage successful is "ours."

ROBERT QUILLEN

~

The secret of happy marriage is simple: just keep on being as polite to each other as you are to your best friends.

ROBERT QUILLEN

~

Something else every couple should save for their old age is their marriage.

IMOGENE FEY

Socrates' marital difficulties are well known. Out of them he coined this sage advice: "By all means marry. If you get a good wife you will become very happy; if you get a bad one you will become a philosopher—and that is good for every man."

LEEWIN B. WILLIAMS

No other human enterprise would have anything of the success marriage enjoys if it were handled so carelessly, so casually, and with so little science.

ERNEST R. GROVES

Another reason for unhappy marriages is that men can't fool their wives like they could their mothers.

It is not marriage that fails, it is people that fail. All that marriage does is show people up.

HARRY EMERSON FOSDICK

You shouldn't criticize your wife's judgment—look who she married!

~

To marry a woman for her beauty is like buying a house for its paint.

~

An ideal wife is any woman who has an ideal husband.

BOOTH TARKINGTON

~

In married life no wife gets what she expected, and no husband expected what he's getting.

THE CHRISTIAN PARENT

S ome people are funny," mused the curbstone
philosoher. "I know a man who had not kissed his
wife for ten years. Then he shot a fellow who did."

A n old lady went to a tombstone-cutter to order
a stone for her husband's grave. After
explaining that all she wanted was a small one with
no frills, she told him to put the words, "To my
husband," in a suitable place.

When the stone was delivered, she saw, to
her horror, this inscription:

"To my husband
In a suitable place."

L & N MAGAZINE

D id you hear about the wife who
cured her husband of his
"have-to-work-late-at-the-office" routine?
She asked him if she could depend on it.

A motorist and his wife hadn't spoken for miles. They'd gotten into a quarrel and neither would budge. Suddenly the man pointed to a mule in a pasture they were passing.

"A relative of yours?" he asked.

"Yes," the wife replied, "by marriage."

~

To keep your marriage brimming
With love in the loving cup,
Whenever you're wrong admit it,
Whenever you're right, shut up.

OGDEN NASH

~

A woman went to a marriage counselor and complained of her husband's overwhelming self-interest. "It was evident from the minute we married," she said. "He wanted to be in the wedding pictures."

IDA ROSE

A man went out with the boys one evening and, before he realized it, the morning of the next day had dawned. He hesitated to call home and talk to his wife. Finally, he hit upon an idea. He telephoned and when his wife answered he shouted, "Don't pay the ransom, Honey—I escaped."

MODERN MATURITY

❧

Husband: "Do you have any idea how many really great people there are in this country?"
    Wife: "No, I don't, but I'm sure it's one less than you think."

❧

How'd you make out in that fight with your wife?"
    "She came crawling to me on her hands and knees."
    "Yeah? What did she say?"
    "Come out from under that bed, you coward!"

R & R MAGAZINE

Business man: "My wife doesn't care how good-looking my secretary is as long as he is efficient."

SUNSHINE

❧

One Sunday afternoon the husband had two radios and the television going all at once to see and hear his favorite sports.

Later his wife said, "Dear, would you explain what the sportscaster meant when he said Carter batted a line drive through the goalposts for a par three?"

SUNSHINE

❧

A couple was sitting in the worship service when the wife suddenly remarked, "Oh, how awful! I forgot to turn off the electric iron before I left home!"

"Don't worry, dear," the husband said cheerfully. "It won't burn long. I just remembered I forgot to turn off the faucet in the bathtub."

GEORGE SWEETING

How much the wife is dearer than the bride.

GEORGE, LORD LYTTLETON

~

Happiness in marriage is not a matter of sentiment; it is a matter of knowledge, ideals, and ethical controls.

A. E. BAILEY

~

A golden wedding is when the couple has gone fifty-fifty.

V

Parentage is a very important profession.

GEORGE BERNARD SHAW

Honor thy father and thy mother: that thy days may be long upon the land which the Lord thy God giveth thee.

EXODUS 20:12

❧

Parents are people who bear children, bore teenagers, and board newlyweds.

❧

Suppose we could give one gift to every child in the world. What should it be? Education? Enough to eat? Freedom from fear? Money? Fun? A career with that all-important sense of worth?

Good as these are there is one thing better. According to those who know, this is a fact: the most favored children in the world are the ones whose parents love each other.

CHARLIE SHEDD

You can't do much about your ancestors, but you can influence your descendants enormously.

~

We parents can often do more for our children by correcting our own faults than by trying to correct theirs.

~

Most parents would willingly follow the biblical counsel to "train up a child in the way he should go" if they could keep their children home long enough.

GRIT

~

Parents wonder why the streams are bitter when they themselves have poisoned the fountain.

JOHN LOCKE

Before I got married I had six theories about bringing up children; now I have six children and no theories.

LORD ROCHESTER

∽

Parents live longer than the children— every day.

∽

A famous pediatrician was asked by a mother what the best time was to put her children to bed.

"While you still have the strength," was the answer.

∽

One of life's pleasantest moments comes when your children get to the age when you don't have to pretend any longer that you know everything.

GRIT

A Parent's Prayer

Oh, heavenly Father, make me a better parent. Teach me to understand my children, to listen patiently to what they have to say, and to answer all their questions kindly. Keep me from interrupting them or contradicting them. Make me as courteous to them as I would have them be to me. May I never punish them for my own selfish satisfaction or to show my power.

Let me not tempt my child to lie or steal. And guide me hour by hour that I may demonstrate by all I say and do that honesty produces happiness.

Reduce, I pray, the meanness in me. And when I am out of sorts, help me, O Lord, to hold my tongue.

May I ever be mindful that my children are children and I should not expect of them the judgment of adults.

Let me not rob them of the opportunity to wait on themselves and to make decisions.

Bless me with the bigness to grant them all their reasonable requests, and the courage to deny them privileges I know will do them harm.

Make me fair and just and kind. And fit me, O Lord, to be loved and respected and imitated by my children. Amen.

ABIGAIL VAN BUREN
(*"Dear Abby"*)

The parents gave their daughter a new car as a birthday present. On the windshield was a card signed, "With love, Mama and Pauper."

~

As a concerned father, I want my girls to attend sex education classes in school. And I want them to go out with boys and enjoy drive-in movies, hayrides, and beach parties. I only ask that they wait until they're old enough. Say about thirty-five.

EDWIN A. ROBERTS, JR.

~

Parents of teens would make great tightrope artists—we've had so much practice. We are always walking that fine line between too-far-away and too-close. We must never be snoopy—curious but always interested, neither square nor yet too hip. We should blend in with the scenery but stand firm as a rock when needed—which is oftener than we may think. We must face temporary closeouts with humor and hope.

HELEN BOTTEL

Anybody who thinks this is a man's world probably isn't a father.

SOCRATES

~

I have chosen him that he may charge his sons and his household after him to follow the directions of the Eternal by doing what is good and right.

GENESIS 18:19
Moffat

~

There was a man who had a wayward son who was constantly getting into trouble. Over and over the father would pay the boy's fine and bring him back home.

One day a neighbor said, "If that were my boy, I would wash my hands of him."

The father replied, "If he were your boy, I would, too."

Fathers who want their children to end up right must walk uprightly themselves.

NAT OLSON

❧

Many a son has lost his way among strangers because his father was too busy to get acquainted with him.

WILLIAM L. BROWNELL

❧

Willy, *longingly* [*to Ben*]: ". . . Dad left when I was such a baby and I never had a chance to talk to him and I still feel—kind of temporary about myself."

ARTHUR MILLER
Death of a Salesman

❧

Some make the mistake of thinking that though fathers are important in the lives of young boys, they are not so necessary in bringing up girls.

This is not true, for the father is the first male a girl encounters in her life, and it is through this contact and through watching the mother relate to her husband that girls experience the first emotions and feelings of the relationship between the sexes.

ANN LANDERS

A great man once said: "In early life I had nearly been betrayed into the principles of atheism, but there was one argument in favor of Christianity I could not refute, and that was the consistent character and example of my own father."

⌇

A minister tells of when he first started in the ministry. His father was also a minister, a very outstanding one. The son dreaded preaching before his father, but there came the day. He preached that day his best sermon and waited for his father's comments.

"Son, that was a great sermon." No criticisms or suggestions, no mention of mispronounced words.

Whenever he preached before his father, the comments he heard were always positive: "You blessed me"—"You preach like a bishop"—and the like.

His father became then even greater in his life, because he knew that what his son needed was confidence—not criticism.

A proud father phoned the newspapers and reported the birth of twins. The girl at the desk didn't quite catch the message.

"Will you repeat that?" she asked.

"Not if I can help it," he replied.

~

A father was walking with his young son. The boy said, "Daddy, what is electricity?"

"I do not really know," said the father. "I never knew much about electricity. All I know about it is that it makes things run."

A little farther on, the boy said, "Daddy, how does gasoline make automobiles go?"

The father replied, "Well, I don't know. I don't know much about motors."

Several more questions followed with much the same result; until at last the boy said, "Gee, I hope you don't mind my asking so many questions."

"Not at all, son," said the father, "You go right ahead and ask. How else will you ever learn anything?"

G od could not be everywhere, and therefore he made mothers.

JEWISH SAYING

~

M aternal love: a miraculous substance which God multiplies as he divides it.

VICTOR HUGO

~

I think it must somewhere be written, that the virtues of mothers shall be visited on their children, as well as the sins of the fathers.

CHARLES DICKENS

~

A n ounce of mother is worth a pound of clergy.

SPANISH PROVERB

He who takes the child by the hand takes mother by the heart.

DANISH PROVERB

~

Let France have good mothers, and she will have good sons.

NAPOLEON BONAPARTE

~

The mother's heart is the child's schoolroom.

HENRY WARD BEECHER

~

A godly mother will point her children to God by the force of her example as much as by the power of her words.

I remember my mother's prayers; they have clung to me all my life.

ABRAHAM LINCOLN

~

By whose preaching were you converted?" a young man was asked. "Not by anyone's preaching, but by my mother's practicing," he answered.

~

A little boy, who was told by his mother that it was God who made people good, responded, "Yes, I know it is God, but Mothers help a lot."

CHRISTIAN GUARDIAN

I don't think there are enough devils in hell to take a young person from the arms of a godly mother.

BILLY SUNDAY

~

A poultry owner in eastern Oregon has a mother hen of whom she is proud. One day a chicken hawk swooped down upon the band of baby fowls of which the old hen was the mother. The hen didn't squawk and run; calling upon her offspring to follow her, she faced the hawk to fight, and so fierce was her onslaught as she buried her bill beneath the hawk's left wing that the hawk seemed surprised and dazed. It feebly rose, flew aimlessly against a clothesline, then dropped into the garden, stone dead. Ordinarily the hen was timid. It was the "mother" in her that rose to the great emergency. How much it means when God says, "as one whom his mother comforteth, so will I comfort you" (Isaiah 66:13).

LOUIS ALBERT BANKS

~

God pardons like a mother who kisses the offense into everlasting forgetfulness.

HENRY WARD BEECHER

A funny phrase
Is 'working mother';
When baby comes,
There is no other!

BERN SHARFMAN

All mothers are physically handicapped. They have only two hands.

When mother, in sheer exasperation,
Is tempted to hand in her resignation,
What adds to her gloom,
Is not knowing to whom!

MAY RICHSTONE

A mother who knows best knows better than to say so.

The quickest way for a mother to get her children's attention is to sit down and look comfortable.

~

A mother was asked: "Which of your children do you love the most?" She replied, "The one who is sick until it gets well, and the one who is away until it gets home."

~

A MOTHER'S PRAYER

Lord, give me patience when wee hands
Tug at me with their small demands.
Give me gentle and smiling eyes;
Keep my lips from hasty replies.
Let not weariness, confusion, or noise
Obscure my vision of life's fleeting joys.
So, when in years to come, my house is still—
No bitter memories its rooms may fill.

Amen.

This is the day and age when we hear a great deal about rights and responsibilities. Everybody acknowledges that mothers have responsibilities—more than their share, most of the time. But who goes on record for a mother's rights?

A mother has a right to own things. You mothers of sons aren't troubled with this very much, but we mothers of daughters find it most difficult to own hosiery, cosmetics, scarves, blouses, etc.

A mother has a right to express an opinion. Most mothers find when they open their mouths that their children say "Oh, Mom!"

A mother has a right to worry . . . whether you are eating the right food, dressing warmly enough, or staying out late and not getting enough sleep . . . whether you are studying enough, especially at the prices the family is paying for tuition . . . whether you are choosing the right kind of companions, whether you are conducting yourselves as honorable and decent ladies and gentlemen.

A mother has a right to be a person. She is entitled to her personal prejudices. She should be allowed to object if the radio is too loud, if the family car is gone too often, if allowances disappear too quickly, and if nobody shows up for meals on time.

A mother should be allowed to be away from home occasionally without hearing an accusing voice bellowing, "Mom, where were you? I called and called!"

Mothers are human beings, after all. None of us is perfect. But most of us try very, very hard.

BETTY MULLINS JONES

In a crowded city a little boy lost his mother. He went in and out of stores and saw ladies carrying packages, but none was his mother. He went to the end of the block where there was a policeman and, pointing to the passing crowd, asked, "Mister, did you happen to see a lady going by without me?"

JOHN R. BROKHOFF

∾

It used to be the custom to picture a mother as white-haired and aproned, busy in the kitchen with dumplings and apple pies and things that smelled so good and tasted so good you'd remember them all your life. Or sometimes she was envisioned in her rocking chair with bifocals and shawl, knitting or sewing or busy with spinning wheel or loom.

Today she's as likely to be slim as a rail . . . a whiz at sky diving, as quick-thinking as a computer and as much at ease the controls of a sports car as with a broom and dust pan or a sink full of dishes.

She rocks the cradle, rules the world, makes dirty little faces shine and unruly little minds nimble. Her work is never done. It's the most important work there is.

RICHARD R. ROBERTS

VI

~

Children are the hands by
which we take hold of heaven.

HENRY WARD BEECHER

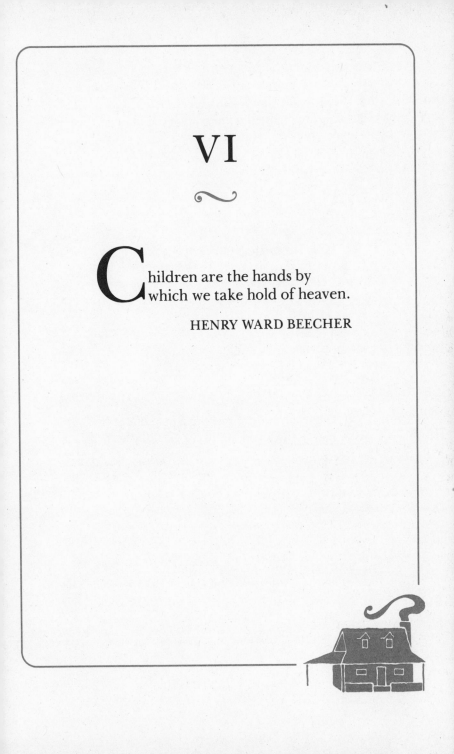

Every child comes into the world with the message that God does not yet despair of man.

TAGORE

❧

A baby is a small member of the family that makes love stronger, days shorter, nights longer, the bank roll smaller, the home happier, clothes shabbier, the past forgotten, and the future worth living for.

❧

A baby has a way of making a man out of his father and a boy out of his grandfather.

ANGIE PAPADAKIS

❧

I love little children, and it is not a slight thing when they, who are fresh from God, love us.

CHARLES DICKENS

I saw tomorrow marching
    On little children's feet;
Within their forms and faces read
    Her prophecy complete.

I saw tomorrow look at me
    From little children's eyes
And thought how carefully we'd teach
    If we were only wise.

ANONYMOUS

Whatever you write on the heart of a child
    No water can wash away.
The sand may be shifted when billows are wild
And the efforts of time may decay.
Some stories may perish, some songs be forgot
But this graven record—time changes it not.
Whatever you write on the heart of a child,
A story of gladness or care
That heaven has blessed or earth has defiled,
Will linger unchangeably there.

SELECTED

If a child lives with criticism,
    he learns to condemn.
If a child lives with hostility,
    he learns to fight.
If a child lives with ridicule,
    he learns to be shy.
If a child lives with shame,
    he learns to feel guilty.
If a child lives with tolerance,
    he learns to be patient.
If a child lives with encouragement,
    he learns confidence.
If a child lives with praise,
    he learns to appreciate.
If a child lives with fairness,
    he learns justice.
If a child lives with security,
    he learns to have faith.
If a child lives with approval,
    he learns to like himself.
If a child lives with acceptance and friendship,
    he learns to find love in the world.

DOROTHY LAW NOLTE

Let thy child's first lesson be obedience, and the second will be what thou wilt.

BENJAMIN FRANKLIN

The right instruction of youth is a matter in which Christ and the whole world is concerned.

MARTIN LUTHER

The training of children is a profession in which we must know how to lose time in order to gain it.

JEAN JACQUES ROUSSEAU

A torn jacket is soon mended, but hard words bruise the heart of a child.

HENRY WADSWORTH LONGFELLOW

The church which neglects its children will have children who neglect the church.

Childhood shows the man as morning shows the day.

JOHN MILTON

We are apt to forget that children watch examples better than they listen to preaching.

ROY L. SMITH

Most of our homes are having this painful contemplation: A child is born in the home and for twenty years makes so much noise we think we can hardly stand it; and then he departs leaving the home so silent that we think we'll go mad.

Children sweeten labours, but they make misfortunes more bitter.

FRANCIS BACON

A CHILD'S BILL OF RIGHTS

The right to the affection and intelligent guidance of understanding parents.

2.   The right to be raised in a decent home in which he or she is adequately fed, clothed, and sheltered.

3.   The right to the benefits of religious guidance and training.

4.   The right to a school program which, in addition to sound academic training, offers maximum opportunity for individual development and preparation for living.

5.   The right to receive constructive discipline for the proper development of good character, conduct, and habits.

6.   The right to be secure in his or her community against all influences detrimental to wholesome development.

7.   The right to the individual selection of free and wholesome recreation.

8.   The right to live in a community in which adults practice the belief that the welfare of their children is of primary importance.

9.   The right to receive good adult example.

NEW YORK YOUTH COMMISSION

Children may tear up a house, but they never break up a home.

~

Birds in their little nests agree;
And 'tis a shameful sight,
When children of one family
Fall out and chide, and fight.

ISAAC WATTS

~

The infinite variety of people's personalities and tastes is something to be marveled at, not frightened of. The luckiest families are those that can take each child on his own merits, enjoying the differences each youngster reveals, and preparing each of them to feel at home in a world of "different" people.

ALICE LOOMER

I am one of the poor abused mothers you've wept about. To a few the word *children* may mean:

Care
Hubbub
Illness
Lack of time
Defeat of talent and ambition
Run-down home
End of fun, extra work
Noise and nagging

To me, the word has many wonderful meanings, including:

Companionship
Hope for a better tomorrow
Inspiration and added interest in my daily life
Love and laughter
Determination to do my best every day
Rewards that can't be measured
Extra fun, extra enthusiasm
Never a dull or lonely moment

JANE K. SHOEMAKER

T here are only two things children will share willingly—communicable diseases and their mother's age.

A policeman noticed a boy with a lot of stuff packed on his back riding a tricycle around and around the block. Finally he asked him where he was going.

"I'm running away from home," the boy said.

The policeman then asked him, "Why do you keep going around and around the block?"

The boy answered, "My mother won't let me cross the street."

~

A little girl was taking an evening walk with her father. Wonderingly, she looked up at the stars and exclaimed: "Oh, Daddy, if the wrong side of heaven is so beautiful, what must the right side be!"

~

A little boy and his daddy were looking at a litter of puppies, planning to buy one, and the daddy asked the boy which one he wanted. The lad pointed to a pup whose tail was wagging furiously and said, "That one with the happy ending."

PRESBYTERIAN LIFE

~

There's nothing so sweet as a girl—
Dainty and tender and whimsical, too
Loving and lovable, eager to please
Questioning, longing, expectant and true
No flower ever fairer than is one of these
There's nothing so sweet as a girl!—

Unless it's a boy!

There's nothing so fine as a boy—
Sturdy and lovable, valiant and strong
Noisy and mischievous, daring and bold
Loyal and faithful to his right or wrong
Caveman and savage, and then knight of old
There's nothing so fine as a boy—

Unless it's a girl!

AUTHOR UNKNOWN

~

The Sunday school teacher asked one little girl if she knew the story of Adam and Eve. "First God created Adam," she said, "and then He looked at him and said, 'I think I can do better,' so he created girls."

There was a little girl, she had a little curl
    Right in the middle of her forehead;
And when she was good, she was very, very good,
    And when she was bad, she was horrid.

HENRY WADSWORTH LONGFELLOW

Little girls are the nicest things that happen to people. They are born with a little bit of angel-shine about them, and though it wears thin sometimes, there is always enough left to lasso your heart—even when they are sitting in the mud, or crying temperamental tears, or parading up the street in Mother's best clothes.

A little girl can be sweeter (and badder) oftener than anyone else in the world. She can jitter around, and stomp, and make funny noises that frazzle your nerves, yet just when you open your mouth, she stands there demure with that special look in her eyes. A girl is Innocence playing in the mud, Beauty standing on its head, and Motherhood dragging a doll by the foot. . . .

Who else can cause you more grief, joy, irritation, satisfaction, embarrassment, and genuine delight than this combination of Eve, Salome, and Florence Nightingale? She can muss up your home, your hair, and your dignity—spend your money, your time, and your patience—and just when your temper is ready to crack, her sunshine peeks through and you've lost again.

Yes, she is a nerve-racking nuisance, just a noisy bundle of mischief. But when your dreams tumble down and the world is a mess—when it seems you are pretty much of a fool after all—she can make you a king when she climbs on your knee and whispers, "I love you best of all!"

ALAN BECK

Between the innocence of babyhood and the dignity of manhood we find a delightful creature called a boy. Boys come in assorted sizes, weights, and colors, but all boys have the same creed: to enjoy every second of every minute of every hour of every day and to protest with noise (their only weapon) when their last minute is finished and the adult males pack them off to bed at night.

Boys are found everywhere—on top of, underneath, inside of, climbing on, swinging from, running around, or jumping to. Mothers love them, little girls hate them, older sisters and brothers tolerate them, adults ignore them, and Heaven protects them. A boy is Truth with dirt on its face, Beauty with a cut on its finger, Wisdom with bubble gum in its hair, and the Hope of the future with a frog in its pocket. . . .

A boy is a magical creature—you can lock him out of your workshop, but you can't lock him out of your heart. You can get him out of your study, but you can't get him out of your mind. Might as well give up—he is your captor, your jailor, your boss, and your master—a freckle-faced, pint-sized, cat-chasing, bundle of noise. But when you come home at night with only the shattered pieces of your hopes and dreams, he can mend them like new with the two magic words, "Hi Dad!"

ALAN BECK

A boy is a noise with some dirt on it.

❧

It is easier and better to build boys than to repair men.

❧

Every boy—down deep in his heart—would like to be a hero—to himself, to his fellows, to people around him. He sometimes likes to picture himself in the limelight—being seen and heard and looked up to—respected and admired. He visualizes himself frequently as a saver of life, as a protector and defender of the weak, as a young man of courage and strength. But most of all he pictures himself as becoming a respected, useful, worthwhile man.

WALTER MacPEAK

~

A FATHER'S PRAYER

Build me a son, O Lord, who will be strong enough to know when he is weak, and brave enough to face himself when he is afraid. One who will be proud and unbending in defeat but humble and gentle in victory.

A son whose wishbone will not be where his backbone should be; a son who will know that to know himself is the foundation stone of knowledge.

Rear him, I pray, not in the paths of ease and comfort but under the stress and spur of difficulties and challenges. Here let him learn compassion for those who fail.

Build me a son whose heart will be clean, whose goal will be high. A son who will master himself before he seeks to master other men. One who will learn to laugh, yet never forget how to weep. One who will reach into the future, yet never forget the past.

And after all these are his, add, I pray, enough of a sense of humor so that he may always be serious, yet never take himself too seriously; a touch of humility, so that he may always remember the simplicity of true greatness; the open mind of true wisdom; the meekness of true strength.

Then, I, his father, will dare to whisper, "I have not lived in vain."

GEN. DOUGLAS MacARTHUR

~

VII

~

K eep true to the dreams of
thy youth!

JOHANN SCHILLER

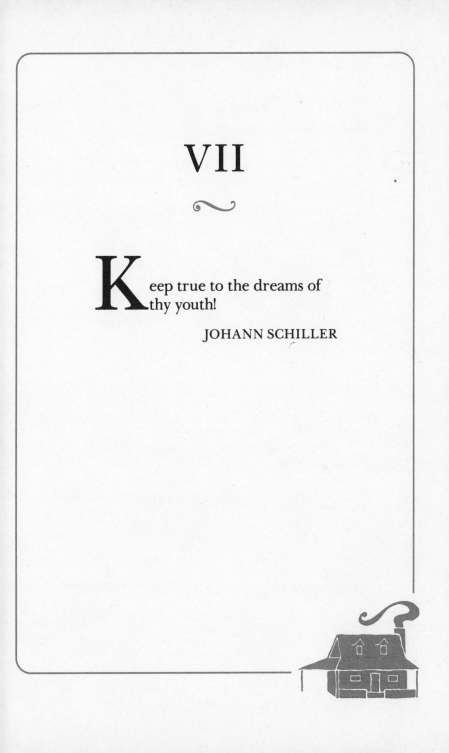

L et no man despise thy youth.

1 TIMOTHY 4:12

~

A ge does not always bring wisdom. Most old people think that because they are old, they have wisdom. Youth keeps the world alive with its dreams, hopes, ambitions.

CLARENCE DARROW

~

T he old say: "I remember when . . ."
The young say: "What's new?"

~

T he destiny of any nation, at any given time, depends on the opinions of its young men under twenty-five.

JOHANN WOLFGANG VON GOETHE

I am just a young man."

In other words, what thousands of men today would like to be!

A potentiality with his face to the East!

A lifetime stretching ahead!

The Book of Life with clean pages to be written on as he may elect! . . .

How many men there are who would gladly give all they possess to have that chance once more!

EDWARD K. BOK

~

The overwhelming majority of young people do NOT go wrong. If they did, civilization would be destroyed. This idea of despairing of the young people is not new.

Let me read the famous words of Socrates, which he spoke 400 years before Christ. He listed the sins of youth as ". . . luxury, bad manners, contempt for authority, disrespect for elders . . . they contradict their parents, they cross their legs, and tyrannize their teachers."

These are the same things that every generation of older people have been saying about youth ever since. But most young people are serious, intelligent, moral, and intend to make something of their lives.

CHARLES L. ALLEN

Teenagers are young people who get too much of everything, including criticism.

SOL KENDON

~

My grandfather in his house of logs
　　Said the young folks are going to the dogs,
His grandfather in the Flemish bogs
　　Said the young folks are going to the dogs,
And his grandfather in his long, skin togs
　　Said the young folks are going to the dogs!
There is but one thing I have to state:
　　We dogs are having a mighty long wait!

ANONYMOUS

~

Youth comes but once, fortunately. You couldn't stand all that abuse for a whole lifetime.

CHANGING TIMES

W hen we are out of sympathy with the young
our work in this world is over.

GEORGE MacDONALD

❧

I believe in teen-agers because they make
mistakes, just as their fathers did.

I believe in teen-agers because they are our
future. They start out clean, eagerly. They want to
win. They do not want to lose.

I believe in teen-agers because they are
growing. They outgrow their clothes, but they
also outgrow their childish ideas, habits, and
childishness. They are dynamic.

I believe in teen-agers because they are a
good investment. I cannot give them much money,
but I can give them a lot of love, understanding,
and concern.

A teen-ager wakes up when he meets
Jesus Christ. Up to that time, his life has been a
protected, cloistered one in which the necessities
have been provided through no effort of his own.
His clothing, food, housing, all have been given
to him by conscientious providers known as
parents. Now that he has come into the age of
decision and maturity of mentality, his horizons
can be unlimited.

J. LESTER HARNISH

W hat do you want when you grow up?" asked the visitor of his host's teenage son.

"I want to be possible," was the boy's quick reply.

"Possible?" said the visitor, perplexed.

"Yes," said the boy. "Every day somebody tells me I'm impossible!"

~

Y ou are only young once, but you can stay immature indefinitely.

GRIT

~

Y outh is the period of building up in habits and hopes and faiths. Not an hour but is trembling with destinies; not a moment, once passed, of which the appointed work can ever be done again, or the neglected blow struck on the cold iron.

JOHN RUSKIN

S o nigh is grandeur to our dust,
    So near is God to man,
When Duty whispers low, "Thou must,"
The youth replies, "I can."

RALPH WALDO EMERSON

T his is not a day when the young listen to
    advice from the old with much grace. In
spite of that, I cannot refrain from giving this wise
word from Anne Bradstreet who lived in the 17th
century:

"Youth is a time of getting,—middle age of
improving,—and old age of spending;

"A negligent youth is usually attended by an
ignorant middle age, and both by an empty old age."

The thing that troubles me the most about
foolish behavior on the part of the young is that,
when these years are spent, they can never be
recovered. Middle age and old age become ignorant
and empty.

BISHOP GERALD KENNEDY

The Teen (not Ten) Commandments:

(1) Stop and think before you drink.

(2) Don't let your parents down—they brought you up.

(3) Be humble enough to obey. You will be giving orders to yourself someday.

(4) At the first moment turn away from unclean thinking—at the first moment.

(5) Don't show off when driving. If you want to race, go to Indianapolis.

(6) Choose a date who would make a good mate.

(7) Go to church faithfully. God gave us a week; give him back an hour.

(8) Avoid following the crowd. Be an engine, not a caboose.

(9) Choose your companions carefully. You are what they are.

(10) Or, even better—keep the original Ten Commandments.

The main problem with teenagers is that they're just like their parents were at their age.

~

Teenage is when your offspring quit asking where they came from and refuse to tell you where they're going!

~

Adolescence is a time of rapid changes. Between the ages of 12 and 17, for example, a parent ages as much as twenty years.

CHANGING TIMES

~

Adolescence is that period when a boy refuses to believe that someday he will be as ignorant as his parents.

A father told his teenage daughter he wanted her home by 11 P.M.

"But Father," she complained, "I'm no longer a child."

"I know," answered her father. "That's why I want you home by 11!"

GOAT

⁓

Father bought a little car,
　He feeds it gasoline,
And everywhere that father goes,
He walks—his son's sixteen.

⁓

My teenage daughter is at that awkward age," one mother said. "She knows how to make phone calls, but she doesn't know how to end them."

I will study and prepare myself, and someday my chance will come.

ABRAHAM LINCOLN

❧

If education can fit youth to face what the world calls failure, it will help them to find what God calls success.

RALPH W. SOCKMAN

❧

Backward, turn backward,
O time in your flight,
And tell me just one thing
I studied last night.

ROBERT BROWN

❧

Adolescent: One who is well informed about anything he doesn't have to study.

A teenager complained to a friend: "My dad wants me to have all the things he never had when he was a boy—including five straight As on my report card."

~

T he dean of a certain school wouldn't allow the star football player to play in the big game coming up Saturday. The coach brought the player into the dean's office and cried: "Why don't you let him play Saturday—we need him!"

"I'll tell you why," snapped the dean. "This is supposed to be a school of learning. All he knows is football, and I'll show you how ignorant he is!"

Then he said to the player: "Tell me, how much is two and two?"

"Seven," came the answer.

With that the coach cried to the dean: "Aw, let him play. After all, he only missed it by one!"

PRACTICAL ENGLISH

Remember now thy Creator in the days of thy youth.

ECCLESIASTES 12:1

~

If the church is to survive it must win and integrate into its life the youth of today.

JESSIE B. EUBANK

~

Youth is the strategic time for laying the foundations for great living, for beginning worthwhile things, and for deciding in favor of God and religion. The great ethical and religious teachers of the race, and all who see life steadily and see it whole, are at one in this view of the matter. It is all right to rejoice in your youth and to thrill to "the wild joy of living," but, as the writer of Ecclesiastes insists, it is well to reflect on the fact of judgment and to remember God in the days of youth. If religion is good only for maturity and age, it is not good enough. If it is good at all, it must be good for all. It is the part of wisdom to seek it in youth.

WILLIAM O. CARRINGTON

C hrist appeals to young people because of their need for love. Everyone needs love, but the need is accentuated in the experience of youth. They cover this need up rather effectively because they are so afraid they won't be loved. But the need is there.

II.   Christ appeals to young people because of their need for forgiveness. I do not know of any group of individuals who get more uptight about their imperfection.

III.   Christ appeals to young people's need for meaning in life. The thing that makes Christ appealing to young people is that he can bring meaning and joy and hope, even in a world like ours. They are attracted by a God who came into this imperfect world and lived in it and brought meaning and hope where there is imperfection and sin.

KENNETH CHAFIN

VIII

Beautiful young people are accidents of nature. But beautiful old people are works of art.

MARJORIE BARSTOW GREENBIE

Cosmetics were used in the Middle Ages; in fact they're still used in the Middle Ages.

～

Middle age is the time of life when your idea of getting ahead is to stay even.

～

Adolescence is when you think you'll live forever. Middle age is when you wonder how you've lasted so long.

～

Middle age is when you're just as young as ever, but it takes a lot more time.

Wouldn't it be terrible if we were born old, and had to look forward to growing young, green, and silly?

~

We are living in a day when young people are encouraged to believe that they are infinitely wiser than their elders. Of course, growing boys and girls have always had a bit of this, but it is rather more so today. It should be remembered that young people have not yet been old, but older people have been young. So older people understand younger people better than younger people understand older people.

J. C. MACAULAY

~

Our greatest obligation to our children and grandchildren is to prepare them to understand and to deal effectively with the world in which they will live—not with the world we have known—or the world we would prefer to have.

GRAYSON KIRK

The importance of grandparents in the life of little children is immeasurable. A young child with the good fortune to have grandparents nearby benefits in countless ways. It has a place to share its joys, its sorrows, to find a sympathetic and patient listener, to be loved.

A child without grandparents can feel the lack of roots and a lack of connectedness. It misses a chance to link up with the past. Questions and answers about the "old days" locate a child historically in his own small world. It provides a sense of inner security and a feeling of belonging.

EDWARD WAKIN

∿

GRANDMA

My grandma likes to play with God,
They have a kind of game.
She plants the garden full of seeds,
He sends the sun and rain.

She likes to sit and talk with God
And knows He is right there.
She prays about the whole wide world,
Then leaves us in His care.

ANN JOHNSON, age 8
in *The Lutheran Standard*

Forty is the old age of youth;
Fifty is the youth of old age.

VICTOR HUGO

~

How old are you? Youth is not a time of life—it is a state of mind!

You are as young as: your faith, your hope, your confidence.

You are as old as: your doubt, your despair, your fear.

H. B. VAN VELZER

~

No period of life, no position or circumstances, has a monopoly on success. Any age is the right age to start doing!

GERARD

To be seventy years young is sometimes far more cheerful and hopeful than to be forty years old.

OLIVER WENDELL HOLMES

No one grows old by living—only by losing interest in living.

MARIE BENTON RAY

Those who love deeply never grow old; they may die of old age, but they die young.

ARTHUR WING PINERO

To avoid old age, keep taking on new thoughts and throwing off old habits.

Hardening of the heart ages people more quickly than hardening of the arteries.

FRANKLIN FIELD

~

Make it a rule never to regret and never to look back. Regret is an appalling waste of time.

KATHERINE MANSFIELD

~

Get over the idea that only children should spend their time in study. Be a student so long as you still have something to learn, and this will mean all your life.

HENRY L. DOHERTY

~

Winter is on my head, but eternal spring is in my heart.

VICTOR HUGO

In youth the days are short and the years are long; in old age the years are short and the days are long.

～

A man who celebrated his fiftieth wedding anniversary recently reports, "A man is always as young as he feels but seldom as important."

～

Age makes you take twice as long to rest and half as long to get tired.

～

To keep young, associate much with young people. To get old in a hurry, try keeping up with them.

One of the most tragic things I know about human nature is that all of us tend to put off living. We are all dreaming of some magical rose garden over the horizon—instead of enjoying the roses that are blooming outside our windows today.

DALE CARNEGIE

❧

To live in hearts we leave behind—is not to die.

THOMAS CAMPBELL

❧

A man has at least a start on discovering the meaning of human life when he plants shade trees under which he knows full well he will never sit.

ELTON TRUEBLOOD

❧

You are young at any age, if you are planning for tomorrow.

When as a child
I laughed and wept—
Time crept!
When as a youth
I dreamed and talked—
Time walked!
When I became
A full-grown man—
Time ran!
Then as with the years
I older grew—
Time flew!
Soon I shall find
As I travel on—
Time gone!

SOURCE UNKNOWN

Age is opportunity no less
Than youth itself, though in another dress
And as the evening twilight fades away
The sky is filled with stars, invisible by day.

HENRY WADSWORTH LONGFELLOW

IX

~

Bゝut now abide faith, hope, love, these three; But the greatest of these is love.

1 CORINTHIANS 13:13,
New American Standard Version

Love is a hammer that will break the hardest heart.

∽

Once when I was away, I received a letter from my six-year-old son. If I should show you that letter and ask, "Is that letter faultless?" you would answer: "No."

"Is it blameless?" Most assuredly.

Love wrote it, love prompted it, love did the best thing possible, under the conditions of that time; but it is not faultless.

By-and-by I may have a letter from that son, better written, better spelled, but none can ever be more blameless than the first letter which came to me.

Your life will not be faultless—but love can live a life which is blameless.

G. CAMPBELL MORGAN

∽

So long as we love, we serve. So long as we are loved by others, I would almost say we are indispensable; and no man is useless while he has a friend.

ROBERT LOUIS STEVENSON

We do not fall in love; we grow in love, and love grows in us.

KARL MENNINGER

~

Love ever gives—
Forgives—outlives—
And ever stands
With open hands.

And while it lives,
It gives,
For this is Love's prerogative—
To give—and give—and give—

JOHN OXENHAM

~

It is love that asks, that seeks, that knocks, that finds, and that is faithful to what it finds.

ST. AUGUSTINE

Human beings generally respond to loving concern. There is more power in a thimbleful of tears than in a barrel of logic.

C. FRANKLIN ALLEE

~

Love means I want you to be.

ST. AUGUSTINE

~

What is it to love? This depends on the maturity level of the individual. For a baby and a small child to love is to long to be taken care of by someone else. For a school child to love is to care for a friend. For a preadolescent to love is to hero worship. For an adolescent to love is simultaneously to be sexually excited by and to idealize a person of the opposite sex. For a young married person to love is to be enveloped in a total physical and spiritual sharing of experience with a mate. For a fully mature individual to love is to be actively concerned with the satisfactions and full flowering of persons other than himself.

W. HUGH MISSILDINE

118

Love is friendship set on fire.

JEREMY TAYLOR

~

The supreme happiness of life is the conviction
of being loved for yourself, or, more
correctly, being loved in spite of yourself.

VICTOR HUGO

~

I guess it all comes down to the fact that you can't
let yourself be loved, unless you love yourself.
And that would make a great title for a
country-western song.

RON WILSON

~

Love can hope where reason would despair.

GEORGE, LORD LYTTELTON

The deepest truth blooms only from the deepest love.

HEINRICH HEINE

Who has not found the heaven below
Will fail of it above.
God's residence is next to mine,
His furniture is love.

EMILY DICKINSON

Faith, like light, should always be simple and unbending; while love, like warmth, should beam forth on every side, and bend to every necessity of our brethren.

MARTIN LUTHER

Man while he loves is never quite depraved.

CHARLES LAMB

He drew a circle that shut me out—
Heretic, rebel, a thing to flout.
But love and I had the wit to win;
We drew a circle that took him in!

EDWIN MARKHAM

Nothing is sweeter than love, nothing more courageous, nothing higher, nothing wider, nothing more pleasant, nothing fuller nor better in Heaven and earth, because love is born of God, and cannot rest but in God, above all created things. Love feels no burden, thinks nothing of trouble, attempts what is above its strength, pleads no excuse of impossibility. . . . It is therefore able to undertake all things, and it completes many things, and warrants them to take effect, where he who does not love would faint and lie down. Love is watchful and sleeping, slumbereth not. Though weary, it is not tired; though pressed, it is not straitened; though alarmed, it is not confounded; but, as a lively flame and burning torch, it forces its way upwards and securely passes all.

THOMAS Á KEMPIS

PERFECT LOVE

Slow to suspect—quick to trust,
Slow to condemn—quick to justify,
Slow to offend—quick to defend,
Slow to expose—quick to shield,
Slow to reprimand—quick to forbear,
Slow to belittle—quick to appreciate,
Slow to demand—quick to give,
Slow to provoke—quick to conciliate,
Slow to hinder—quick to help,
Slow to resent—quick to forgive.

HERALD OF HOLINESS

∽

I believe that love is the greatest thing in the world; that it alone can overcome hate; that right can and will triumph over might.

JOHN D. ROCKEFELLER, JR.

∽

Love is not love
Which alters when it alteration finds,
Or bends with the remover to remove.

WILLIAM SHAKESPEARE

I never knew a night so black
Light failed to follow on its track.
I never knew a storm so gray
It failed to have its clearing day.
I never knew such bleak despair
That there was not a rift, somewhere.
I never knew an hour so drear
Love could not fill it full of cheer!

JOHN KENDRICK BANGS

Love has many ways of expressing itself, but in
general the ways are two—the practical and
the sentimental. Which is the higher and better way?
It is merely a question of appropriateness under the
circumstances. Love must express itself very often
in coal, and cornmeal, and salt pork, and clothes.
But let it not be concluded that love may not express
itself in acts of pure sentiment. The soul has needs.
Sympathy and tenderness and friendship are just as
real and more enduring, than coal and wood.
Sometimes a flower is more important than flour;
sometimes a word of cheer is better than gold.

FERRAL

~

The Lord bless thee and
keep thee;
The Lord make his face to shine
upon thee
and be gracious unto thee;
The Lord lift up his countenance
upon thee,
and give thee peace.

NUMBERS 6:24–26

~

ACKNOWLEDGMENTS

~

Every effort has been made to trace the ownership of copyrighted material used in this book and to secure permission for its use. Should there be any inadvertent error or omission, the compiler and editor will be pleased to make the necessary corrections in future printings. Thanks are due for permission to use the following copyrighted material:

Selection by Patricia Ward and Martha Stout on page 22, from *Christian Women at Work* by Patricia Ward and Martha Stout. Copyright © 1981 by The Zondervan Corporation. Used by permission.

Selection by Elton and Pauline Trueblood on page 24, from *The Recovery of Family Life,* Harper & Row, 1953.

Selection by George W. Humphreys on page 48, from *Rainbows: The Book of Hope.* Used by permission of Brownlow Publishing Company, Ft. Worth, Texas.

Selection by Leewin B. Williams on page 50, from *Encyclopedia of Wit, Humor and Wisdom.* Abingdon Press, 1949. Used by permission.

Selection by Ogden Nash on page 53, "A Word to Husbands," from *I Wouldn't Have Missed It* by Ogden Nash. Copyright © 1962 by Ogden Nash. By permission of Little, Brown and Company. Also from *Marriage Lines, Notes of a Student Husband.* Reprinted by permission of Curtis Brown Ltd. on behalf of the Estate of Ogden Nash. Copyright © 1964 by Ogden Nash.